RON ERWIN

1

Grizzly bear cubs are born in the middle of the winter, in snow-covered dens, to sluggish, inactive mothers. Born in litters of one to four cubs, and weighing about half a kilogram each (about the size of a chipmunk), the tiny cubs have little hair on their bodies, no teeth and just enough strength to snuggle up against their mother's body to keep warm and suckle milk. Their eyes won't open until they are about three weeks old. However, there won't be much to see until the new family ventures out of the den weeks later in April or early May. By this time the cubs weigh about three to four kilograms each and are more than ready to run, jump and play, experimenting with their newfound freedom.

TONY NEWLIN

2

Grizzly cubs are seldom more than a few hundred metres from their mother once the denning season is over. While the mother bear is very attentive and focussed on her babies, many factors affect their survival, and most cubs do not reach adulthood. Their mother must not only protect them and show them how to cope with danger, but also teach them what to eat and where and how to find their food. Aside from starvation and disease, one of the greatest risks to a mother's cubs is the adult male grizzly bear. Theories as to why the male bear kills its own kind include the need for food, the desire to create a breeding opportunity with the mother and the need to reduce competition for common territory.

MARK NEWMAN

When grizzly bears emerge from their dens, food is localized and hard to come by. Grizzlies require a very high calorie intake because of their size. Once the mother has regained her strength and is ready to leave the den for the season, she and her cubs will travel to areas where there are carcasses of hoofed animals, such as elk and moose, to feed on. Later on in the spring, the family will concentrate on plants and roots for nourishment and by summer they are eating berries. More than 75 per cent of the grizzly's diet consists of vegetation, such as berries, flowers, grasses, herbs, tubers, roots and nuts. The remainder is made up of animal matter, including fish, ants, honey and a variety of small mammals.

After about two and a half years, sometimes more, the grizzly cubs will leave their mother and venture out on their own. As adolescents, the bears are still in grave danger and must become instantly self-sufficient if they are to stay alive and well. After at least two full winters with their mother, they must now find sufficient food on their own to build up their fat reserves to last over a long winter away from her. Young female bears will not reproduce until they are six or seven years of age. Once mature, they will reproduce every four years, on average, and the cycle of bringing beautiful baby cubs into the wonderful world of the Canadian Rockies will continue.

THOMAS KITCHIN

Each year, a dominant pair of grey wolves will produce four to eight wolf pups. These pups will grow to be the largest dogs of the wild dog family, weighing 50 to 70 kilograms. Despite their name, these large beauties can have fur of many colours other than grey, from white to black and every shade of cream, beige and brown in between. To many people, the howl of the wolf symbolizes the sound of the wilderness. The wolf's intelligence is displayed through this characteristic, as the call can mean many different things. The howl is sometimes a signal to reassemble the pack; it is also a way to keep in touch, a territorial cry or simply a sociable call or expression of happiness.

TERRY PARKER/VIEWPOINTS WEST

The red fox's wariness and keen senses have earned it a reputation for cleverness. The fox lives in a burrow or small cave and feeds mainly on rodents, such as mice and rabbits; it also eats insects, frogs, fish, carrion and berries. To catch rodents, it leaps up into the air, then pounces on its prey. The upper parts of the red fox's body are reddish yellow; the under parts and tip of the tail are white, and the feet and lower forelegs are black. A full-grown male fox is about 104 centimetres long, including its 40-centimetre bushy tail. Among the calls of the fox are a yapping bark and a shrill howl. The female fox, called a vixen, utters a piercing yelp at mating time. She bears her litter of three to nine pups in the spring.

RON ERWIN

Pregnant beavers give birth to one to eight kits in the late spring. Each beaver community consists of a mated pair and their kits, as well as last year's offspring. The young leave the community in their third spring. The beautiful beaver is, of course, a symbol of Canada. Its rise to fame started, ironically, with the beaver-fur hat fashion fad. During the peak of the fur trade, 100,000 beaver pelts made their way to Europe each year. As a result, the Canadian beaver was close to extinction in the mid-19th century. Luckily, silk hats became the rage and the beaver lived to become an official emblem of Canada in 1975. The most notable features of the beaver are that they live in lodges, build dams and have large, flat tails.

BYRON JORJORIAN

The hoary marmot is the largest of all North American squirrels. Females give birth to four to five young every second spring. However, it takes two full summers before the young reach full size and can venture out on their own. The full-size marmot is about twice the size of a groundhog, approximately five to six kilograms in weight and one metre in length. The marmot can be heard producing a loud, shrill whistle whenever it senses the slightest hint of a predator. The hoary marmot is also known for padding itself with a layer of fat and hibernating for seven to eight months of the year to avoid the snow that covers the meadows in the Canadian Rockies where it lives.

PAUL HEPPNER/WILDERNESS WEST IMAGES

The large, long-winged hawk known as the osprey is a great Canadian hunter. It is a treat to watch the osprey hunt for fish, on which it subsists almost entirely. It will dive from the air, hitting the water with a resounding splash, and in some cases even disappear beneath the surface momentarily, then fly away with its catch. The osprey builds its nest with a view of the water in mind. It can be spotted high up on cliffs, telephone poles, the sides of bridges and in tall trees. The female usually lays three eggs, which are incubated for five weeks before hatching hungry chicks. After only 10 weeks or so, the young birds have all their flight feathers and are ready to begin their training to fly and hunt.

RONN MARRATEA

The bald eagle is a majestic bird with striking features. It is a favourite with bird watchers, perhaps because it is the only North American bird of prey with a solid white head, neck and tail. However, it is not born with these features. After laying one to three brownish, speckled eggs, either both parents, or just the female, incubate the eggs, which hatch to uniformly brown or mottled brown and white chicks. The striking white features increase with successive plumages. The eagle's nest is most often seen near the top of a tree and usually is quite large since it may be used for many years. The chicks remain in the nest for up to 100 days and are fed by their mother.

GAIL SHUMWAY

The ground squirrel can be identified easily by its frequently assumed upright posture. It is also recognizable by its plump body and its quick, quivering tail, which is not long and bushy like that of the common tree squirrel. The ground squirrel inhabits open plains, where it lives in burrows. It opts for hibernation during the winter when its environment turns harsh and potentially deadly. This rodent feeds on a variety of plants and seeds. The mating season begins in late winter and the young are usually born in the early spring. The babies do not have any hair or teeth and are virtually blind for the first six to eight weeks. A second litter can be born in mid summer, if there is an adequate food supply.

DUANE ROSENKRANZ

Litters of four or five young chipmunks are born each summer. When the young are full grown, they will weigh only 50 grams. These cute little animals are recognized by their familiar stripes, which run from the tip of the nose to the rump. They like to live near creeks and streams, in open forests and on rocky ledges. The chipmunk uses its front paws, which look like tiny human hands, to stuff its cheeks full of its favourite seeds. Once its cheeks are full, it will retreat to a sheltered place before eating. These little friends have a lot of nervous energy that keeps them moving, which could be a blessing since larger animals, such as weasels, hawks, owls and coyotes, prey on both young and adult chipmunks.

ROBERT M. ATKINS

In the spring, the cow (adult female) moose gives birth to one or two calves, weighing between 10 and 15 kilograms each. These babies will grow to be the largest members of the deer family, weighing in excess of 500 kilograms and reaching three metres in length and two metres in height at the shoulder. The moose's long slim legs look almost unable to support the large being above; however, these spindly legs allow the moose to move as swiftly as it does. Bulls (adult males) have antlers, which drop off in the middle of the winter and regrow each year. It is the bulls with the largest antlers that have the right to mate with cows. Vicious battles, called rutting, occur to determine this supremacy.

The undisputed king of the antler world is known for its beautiful mating call. The otherwise quiet animal breaks the silence of the forest with his call for a mate. Once a cow answers they call back and forth until they find each other. When the calves are born, they do not have protective camouflage patterns; however, they have a very aggressive and protective mother. The main causes of death in the moose include parasitic liver flukes, being hit by trains and motor vehicles, and being attacked by wolves and elk. The moose's diet in the winter is derived from mixed forests and includes twigs of willow, aspen and red osier dogwood. The summer months send the moose in search of water plants in the low-lying marshlands. They are also fond of salt and enjoy roadside mineral licks.

MURRAY O'NEILL/VIEWPOINTS WEST

This graceful, beautiful, but timid animal is identifiable by its white tail, which is erect and flared when the deer is startled or alert.
The white-tailed deer is extremely adaptable and is the most widespread deer in Canada. It thrives regardless of conditions, eating twigs, buds and the leaves of aspen, red osier dogwood and other deciduous shrubs and trees. One or two fawns are produced in the spring. They are scentless and rusty brown or chestnut coloured with dappled white spots on their coats, which helps them blend in with their surroundings.
Once they are adults, their coats will be reddish-brown in the summer and greyish-brown in the winter. Their enemies include the wolf, bear, coyote, lynx, cougar and larger members of the weasel family.

BARRETT & MACKAY

The wonderful woodland caribou has many interesting features. Its large hooves are split so the caribou can walk on snow and ice without sinking. This is handy, since its habitat includes Arctic tundra, as well as coniferous forest. The caribou also has a double thick fur coat; the outer guard hairs are shed in the summer. Brown to dark brown in colour, caribou have whitish manes. Both the cows and bulls grow antlers. Babies grow their first antlers at only five months of age. Born at the end of the spring season, the baby caribou's first few hours of life are its most dangerous time. While it is quick on its feet immediately after birth, if it cannot keep up with the herd, it could be eaten by wolves.

BARRETT & MACKAY

The bighorn sheep is a symbol of Canada's Rocky Mountains. Perhaps its prehistoric-looking horns add to its noble appearance among the giant mountains. The sheep are, in fact, descendants of mammals that evolved two to three million years ago. Stately horns are not its only impressive feature; the bighorn sheep is also an agile mountain climber. It has unique, concave hoofs that separate into halves and spread over sharp rocks. Even the newborn lambs are quick on their feet and enjoy dashing about the rocky hillsides. The ewe (female sheep) gives birth to one or two tiny lambs per year. These incredibly cute babies are preyed upon by some of the wild's most dangerous predators, including cougars, wolves, bears and coyotes.

PAUL HEPPNER/WILDERNESS WEST IMAGES

The mountain goat is a truly Canadian alpinist, moving on its highly flexible hooves up and down sheer cliff faces with utter ease and grace. Suction-like cups on the bottoms of its hooves give the goat amazing dexterity. It is more at home on cliffs and rocky terrain than on flat land, which helps it escape its many dangerous enemies, but also puts it at increased risk of falling victim to rock slides and avalanches. This creature actually isn't a goat at all, but is related to the antelope family. It sports a long, fine, white wooly coat that keeps it warm even on the coldest day or the most exposed mountaintops. Courtship begins in late fall and extends into early winter. Then in June, one or two fast-learning kids are born.

One of the elk's distinguishing characteristics is its trumpet-like call. These dark-brown beauties have lighter-coloured rump patches, short tails and dark-brown manes. The bulls have antlers, which are protected by a velvety covering until it is rutting season, when the covering is shed and the antlers calcify into hard bone. Both the bugle call and the antlers play a large part in the mating season. The male uses the bugle to attract females into a harem for mating and also to challenge other males, which usually results in an antler-to-antler confrontation. Females give birth to one or two calves in late May or early June each year. The newborns have a light-brown coat with white spots for camouflage protection.

PAUL HEPPNER/WILDERNESS WEST IMAGES

Coyotes, thought by some experts to be monogamous, operate as a family. They breed each winter and give birth in April or May. Four to eight pups will be born in a hollowed-out den. The male forages for food to feed his mate and new family. The pups receive regurgitated food from spring to autumn, when they will be full grown and able to go out hunting on their own. They will reach sexual maturity by the following winter. The coyote hunts in a team for larger game and alone for smaller prey. Its solitary hunting technique is fascinating to watch: it stalks small prey using a stiff-legged stance and then pounces on the victim with all four feet.

PAUL HEPPNER/WILDERNESS WEST IMAGES

The largest wild cat in Canada, the mountain lion (also known as the cougar or puma) reaches a total length of 2.5 metres and weighs 70 kilograms as an adult. This elusive animal has no natural enemies. It moves around continuously, and can cover up to 50 kilometres in one day. The females can give birth to two to four kittens at any time of the year. Once born, the kittens stay with their mother for more than a year. Except when mating, the mountain lion lives a solitary existence. It is seldom seen, as it lives a secret life in the undisturbed wild lands of the Canadian Rockies. It prefers mountainous terrain and dense boreal forest – the same habitat as its primary prey, the mule deer.

The beautiful Canada lynx is identifiable by the prominent ruff around its face and by its pointed ears, which are tipped with long "pencils" of black hair. The lynx is a true Canadian with a natural ability to walk on snow - its large paws act as snowshoes, making it an efficient hunter year round. The lynx is not often seen because of its secretive nature. It is shy and solitary except when the females are with their kittens. Pregnant cats will have a litter of one to five blind kittens, born in a den, in the late spring. The kittens will stay with their mother for one winter and venture out on their own in the spring. Once full grown, the lynx is similar in size to a large house cat, weighing approximately 10 kilograms.

Often called the wildcat, the bobcat looks a lot like its cousin, the lynx, but has shorter legs and can be distinguished by the black bars on its tail. While it thrives in virtually any surroundings, it prefers less snow and more rough and rocky terrain, caves and ledges. It likes to den under fallen logs or in the root mass of a fallen tree – as long as it is dry and safe. A mother cat will have two or three kittens in the spring. Once the babies are weaned, their mother will catch live prey, such as mice, and bring it to the den so the kittens can practice their hunting skills. When the fall arrives, the kittens, now half their eventual adult weight, will leave their mother.

BJORN JORJORIAN

This beautiful owl is recognizable by its tufted head and its yellow eyes. The small screech owl begins breeding in March and nests in natural cavities or woodpecker holes in trees. The incubation period for the eggs is approximately 29 days. The young owls grow to an adult size of 20 to 25 centimetres tall, and weigh 170 to 226 grams. It is only the baby screech owls that actually make a screeching sound. Adults have two calls. The first call, "Toot, toot, toot toot toot toot ...," accelerates in tempo, similar to a bouncing ball. The second call is a trill. The owl eats just about anything it can catch – mostly small mammals – but also hunts for insects, reptiles, amphibians and small birds.

RON ERWIN

The beautiful and symbolic Canada goose is a familiar favourite. It is known for its famous "V" formation when flying. As each goose flaps its wings it creates an updraft for the birds that follow. By flying in a "V" formation, the entire flock of geese has a 71 per cent greater flying range than if each bird flew alone. One fact that is not as well known, but that further endears the Canada goose to humans, is that these birds often mate for life. In fact, research shows that the goose can pine to death at the loss of its mate. Geese are devoted parents and never leave their goslings unguarded. If a goose is ever aggressive, it's because it is protecting its young.

DUANE ROSENKRANZ

Did you know that loons lay only two eggs? This is because their body size and physiology do not allow them to produce any more than two eggs at once. Loon eggs are very large – approximately the size of one and a half tennis balls. If a loon were to lay more than two eggs, it would need a larger body to be able to hold them inside. Since loons work on laying one egg at a time, they usually lay the two eggs one day apart, which results in the eggs hatching one day apart. Another good reason for the loon to produce only two eggs at a time is the loon's life span. These majestic birds can live up to 30 years, which is a long time compared to most birds. Therefore, hatching only two chicks prevents overpopulation.

ROLF KOPFLE

Big, magical, beautiful polar bears mate out on the ice in April and May. The fertilized egg, however, does not implant and begin to develop until late September or early October. The fuzzy little cubs are born sometime between late November and early January and weigh just 600 grams each. The cubs are helpless at birth and the family remains in the den until late March or early April. While twins are most common, a mother may have one to four cubs per litter. The cubs will remain with their mother for more than two years and will grow to an adult size of 500 to 600 kilograms. Females will have their first litter at the age of five or six.

MIKE MACRI/MASTERFILE

30

Despite its name, the black bear actually can boast a coat in a variety of colours. There are brown black bears, white black bears, and even "blue" glacier black bears. The black bear has shorter, more curved claws than does the grizzly bear. This provides it with the ability to climb trees with great skill. A sow (female bear) will often encourage her cubs to climb a tree when danger is present. They have a characteristic way of climbing trees, mostly using their front claws to pull them up and hold on. The diet of these interesting bears consists of almost anything. They are opportunistic feeders that eat a varied diet of mostly roots, berries, nuts, insects and fish.

PAUL HEPPNER/WILDERNESS WEST IMAGES

Bears have one of the slowest reproduction rates of any land mammal in North America. Female black bears, sexually mature by three to five years of age, give birth to an average of two cubs every other year. While breeding occurs from May through July, the fertilized ovum floats freely in the uterus for around six months before implanting and continuing to develop. The cubs, weighing less than one kilogram, are born in January or February, when the mother is still in hibernation. The cubs are blind and hairless and stay with their mother until their second spring. The natural life span of the black bear can be 25 years or more in the wild; however, a large percentage of Canadian black bears die at the hands of humans, from gunshots, at an average age of just six years.

TERRY PARKER/VIEWPOINTS WEST